1 MONTH OF
FREE
READING

at
www.ForgottenBooks.com

ISBN 978-0-260-45201-6
PIBN 10949111

SPEECH

OF

HIS EXCELLENCY

LEVI LINCOLN,

DELIVERED BEFORE

THE LEGISLATURE,

JUNE 6, 1826.

———

TOGETHER WITH

DOCUMENTS,

REFERRED TO THEREIN.

———

BOSTON:
TRUE AND GREENE, STATE PRINTERS.

·············

1826.

SPEECH.

Gentlemen of the Senate, and
Gentlemen of the House of Representatives.

It is with animating considerations of encouragement to renewed and devoted exertions in the public service, that I find myself sustained by the confidence of my Fellow-Citizens, in the integrity of the motives to my official conduct, during the past year, and it is with the deepest sense of obligation to increased diligence, impartiality, and a regard to the public interest, imposed by the expression of this confidence, in my re-election, that I again enter upon the discharge of the duties of this high station. In an administration of government, resting for support upon popular opinion, it is hardly to be expected, that any course of general policy will meet with entire approbation; nor in the free and voluntary exercise of the right of suffrage, is it reasonably to be looked for, that the personal character and qualifications of a candidate for public favor, will be universally acceptable. —Least of all, did the individual, who is now permitted the honor of addressing you, hope for more than a generous indulgence to unintentional error, and the exercise of a candid judgment upon the principles and measures, which the responsibility of his situation and his conscience required him, faithfully and fearlessly, to avow and to pursue.

The short period which has elapsed since the close of the unusually laborious session of the last Legislature, has furnished few new subjects of public interest, for Executive communication, and the invariable custom of this Government, sanctioned by considerations of general convenience, dispenses with the devotion of much time to the concerns of ordinary legislation, at the present season of the year. The government being fully organized, the wishes and interests of our constituents, will probably be best satisfied, by a preparatory disposition of measures for more leisure attention, at the winter session, and will leave you at liberty to consult your personal accommodation, in conforming to the usual practice, by an early adjournment. I have pleasure in informing you, that I know of no business, which will particularly interfere with such an arrangement, in the exercise of your discretion.

Although these suggestions are respectfully made from a view to the general condition of the Commonwealth, in the common course of the administration of its affairs, yet, they will not, I trust, be regarded as the manifestation of any indifference or of change of opinion, in reference to the advancement of those high objects of public improvement,

which have heretofore been presented for legisla-
tive consideration. Indeed, further inquiry and
reflection, with extended means of information,
have but strengthened the opinion, that the important interests of the people can only be preserved,
and the honour and prosperity of the State promoted, by a system of Governmental enterprize, and
liberality, in accordance with the spirit of the age,
and commensurate with the opportunities which
the bounty of nature and human genius offer to
their indulgence. While all around is in a state of
advancement, can Massachusetts alone remain stationary, without prejudice? Are stupendous works
of public improvement to be elsewhere construct-
ed, opening new lands to settlement, new markets
to population, rewarding the labours of industry,
pouring riches into the treasury of states, and creating lasting resources for the support of civil government, and for the encouragement of the noblest
institutions of learning and the arts, and this ancient Commonwealth, in indifference and inertness,
suffer nothing from the comparison? Not so was
the forecast of our wise and clear-sighted ancestors,
even in the earliest periods of their Colonial and
Provincial history. Whatever tended to distin-
guish their condition above that of others, to improve the prospects of the future, to secure to the
generations of their posterity a great and lasting
benefit, was anxiously and perseveringly pursued;
and for most of the peculiar blessings of which we
are now in the enjoyment, we are indebted to their

enlightened views of the public good, and their
disinterested devotion to public objects. Unheeding
all personal gratifications, they looked forward to
the greatness of the people, of whom they were to
become the progenitors. In self-denial and suffer-
ing, and of their pittance of worldly substance, they
laid deep the foundations of national strength and
glory. To the churches and the schools, and to
the permanent improvement of the condition of society, they applied the utmost of their limited
means. With them, every thing was for the common weal, for the hope of the future, for a better
and brighter condition to those who should come
after them. If their example be not a reproach to
the indulgence and supineness of the present day,
still, upon what shall we rest for proof of its wor-
thiest imitation! If *they* planted the free schools
of Massachusetts, shall not *we* cherish the cause of
learning, with our kindest care? If *they* founded
institutions of civil government, for the promotion
of the general welfare, shall *we* not improve them,
to advance the best interests of the age in which
we live, and in our day also, add something of value,
to the inheritance of those who shall succeed to
us? These inquiries belong to public men. It is
in accordance with the genius of a popular Government, that the constituted agents of the people
execute the public will, nay even, that often, *by
anticipation*, they take the responsibility of its ultimate approval, in measures which are clearly within the delegated authority, and are suggested by

the sound dictates of a liberal and enlightened
judgment. The intelligence of the people is not
so much exercised in the direction of precise acts,
as the expression of general principles, and the
mode in which these are most efficaciously to be
illustrated, is usually submitted, with a generous
confidence, to the discretion of those whom they
voluntarily appoint, to represent and to act for
them.

Among the many advantages resulting from a
frequent recurrence of elections, is the knowledge
which is thus obtained of public sentiment, upon
subjects, which have previously engaged official attention. Since the interesting discussions of the
last Legislature, upon the general topics of education, and of a system of measures in relation to the
resources and internal improvements of the Commonwealth, an opportunity has been afforded for
an expression of the opinions which are entertained by the great body of the people. Coming as
you now recently do, Gentlemen, from every part
of the State, it cannot be difficult to determine upon
measures, which the interests of the community require, and your Fellow Citizens are prepared to sus-
tain. It becomes my duty, respectfully to invite
your deliberations upon such of them as were postponed for further consideration, and your attention
to others, which have peculiar application to the
character of the times and the existing circumstances of the Commonwealth.

Of the most important of the referred business, was the proposition for the establishment of a Seminary of practical Arts and Sciences. A Committee of the House of Representatives having been charged with a revision of this subject, it will probably be addressed to you, under the favorable circumstance of their intelligent expositions. It must be worthy of serious regard, that the means of instruction should keep pace with the increased and increasing population of the State, and are, at all times, wisely adapted to the pursuits and requirements of the people. The system of education, as now supported by the provisions of law, has but little changed with all the astonishing changes which a half century of national independence, of vicissitude from poverty and privation to public and private prosperity, wealth and luxury, have produced. Whatever improvement has been made, is rather in the character of the books used in instruction, than in the manner of imparting it, or the branches of learning which are taught. The business of Society urgently demands great alterations in these particulars. New channels of business, new interests and objects, and other and different capacities for their proper management, require a conformity in the course of preparatory education. The qualifications of Instructors deserve much more of care and attention. To the great honor and happiness of the Commonwealth, this employment has become an extensively desirable and lucrative occupation. It may be safely computed, that the number of male Teachers engaged by the Towns annually, for the whole or parts of the year, does not fall short, of *twenty five hundred* different individuals, to which, if the number of female instructors and those employed in private schools be added, the aggregate would amount to *many thousands.* Knowledge in the art of governing, and a facility in communicating instruction are attainments in the teacher, of indispensable importance to proficiency, by the pupil. These talents are as much to be acquired by education, as are the sciences themselves. It will well merit the consideration of the Legislature when discussing the expediency of the institution of the proposed Seminary, whether provision for the preparation of a class of men to become the instructors of youth in public Schools, in branches of learning, adapted to the present condition and wants of the Country, is not among the highest of the inducements to the measure, and should be an object of primary and definite arrangement, in its adoption.

. The difference of opinion which existed between the two branches of the Legislature, the last year, left undetermined the expediency of a modification of the laws relating to the personal liabilities of corporators in Manufacturing establishments, and renders proper a recurrence to the subject, on this occasion. The number of Corporations, already created, and the immense amount of capital employed in their operation, must prevent the pos-

2

sibility, hereafter, of a successful competition with them in business by individual means, and presents the single enquiry, whether these public establishments can advantageously be multiplied and encouraged. The period has long since passed in which the manufacturing interest could be regarded as unfavourable to commerce, or inconsistent with the prosperity of an agricultural people. Domestic fabrics now furnish the means of extensive trade, and the best markets for the products of the soil are found at the doors of our own workshops. The surprising influence of these institutions, in promoting the general improvement of the Country, may be witnessed wherever they are situated. Look but to the villages of Lowell and of Ware, places where the very wastes of nature, as if by the magic of machinery, have been suddenly converted into scenes of busy population, of useful industry, and of wealth! Regard the effect, in a financial point of view, upon the resources of the Government! The former valuation of the towns of which the sites of those villages were, but recently, the mere by-places, hardly exceeded the amount of property, which has been thus artificially created! At the same time, the neighbouring estates have appreciated, the value of farms has been enhanced and their cultivation encouraged, by an increased demand for their produce. The physical force of the State is strengthened, by the organization of additional corps of militia, from an augmented population,—and its moral condition

improved, by affording occupation to a class of poor
and dependant families, which before were in idle-
ness, for want of the means of employment, and in
ignorance from a denial of opportunities for instruction. Let it not be said, that these results show,
that there is no occasion for the proposed modification of the laws. Many and great as are the improvements already made, there is yet ample room
for their extension. However little, those men
who are engaged in the existing establishments
may have heeded their personal liabilities, or however fortunate or confident they may be in their
present associations, it will not be denied, that there
are numerous others, provident, and discerning, and
enterprizing capitalists too, who are deterred from
participating in the manufacturing business of the
Commonwealth, solely, by the provisions of the
Statutes. Else, from what cause has it arisen, that
large sums have been invested, by citizens of Massachusetts, in the manufactories of the neighbouring States of New-Hampshire and Maine.—Was
it, that upon the banks of our Rivers, no unoccu-
pied place could be found for the location of their
work-shops, or that in the current of the waters no
sufficient power could be acquired to propel their
machinery? Or was it not rather, that the Statute
Books of those Governments, regarding only the
responsibilities of Corporations for credits which
Corporations only obtained, impose no individual
liabilities, by reason of the smallest proportion of
interest, to the payment of Corporate debts, with-

out limit in amount or time of demand, even to the peril of the ruin of private fortune, and of the imprisonment of person? The money which has thus been sent from the Commonwealth, if it had been expended upon similar objects within it, would have added thousands to her population, and hundreds of thousands to her pecuniary resources. This language may be thought more earnest than the subject will justify, but it has been impelled by a strong sense of official duty, and pertains to the expression of those views of public policy, which deeply regard the substantial and permanent prosperity of the State.

By an act of the last session creating the Salem Mill Dam Corporation, the Legislature have already departed from the provisions of the general statute, and expressly sanctioned one of the principles of modification, which has been recommended, that of the limitation, as to time, of the liabilities of individuals after they shall cease to be members of Corporations. Let this principle be equally applied to Stockholders in all Manufacturing Companies, and the extent in the amount of their responsibility be rendered certain, and as much as is consistent with the public security, and all that is desirable, will probably be effected.

But at least there is one feature in the present laws, which if there be no other occasion should induce to their revision. In their practical operation, they now tend to infinite circuity of action, and this effect I have heretofore professionally witnessed.

The Corporator who pays the debt of his Corporation, thereby becomes its creditor. With his process for indemnity, he may fasten, for the whole amount upon the property or person of either of his associates, and this one in turn, for redress, may again recur to the former. The liabilities and the remedies of parties may thus be made perpetually to alternate, or at their election, pass in endless circuity, the round of all the Corporators, and remain forever unsatisfied. If the principle of the personal liability of the members of Corporations is to be preserved, it would seem wise to provide, that, as between themselves, the rule which governs in the case of Co-partners, should be adopted, and that he who discharges the joint debt should look to the joint fund, or have his personal resort to his associates for contribution only, according to their respective proportions of interest.

There is yet another subject of high public concernment, which has heretofore been addressed to the attention of the Legislature, and which, on this occasion, I approach with much solicitude. It is that which relates to the construction of works for promoting and facilitating inter-communication between different and distant places, from the remote extremes to the capital of the State. The opinions of enlightened, discerning, and instructed men, have been sufficiently strong, in other parts of our country, to subject to the test of unerring experience, all speculations upon the operation and results of the accomplishment of similar objects. Through the whole extent of the United States, in various assemblages of citizens, in Congress, and in the Halls of State Legislation, a general sentiment has been declared, favorable to measures for improving the communication between the interior and the sea board, and for expediting the transportation of merchandize and produce to their respective markets.

In *what manner*, and *at what time*, Massachusetts is to profit of the advantages, which such facilities afford, is with the wisdom of the Legislature to decide. It becomes not the respect, which I bear to this Department of the Government, importunately to urge personal opinions upon their adoption. On former occasions these have been distinctly expressed. It unfortunately however, seems to be misunderstood by some, that a *precise* and *exclusive* character of improvement has been contemplated, and a definite object, and that not the most encouraging, selected for the first experiment. Nothing has been further from the intention of the Executive. The great subject of internal improvement, as applicable to the interests of this Commonwealth, was presented for consideration. Whatever was the mode suggested in which this might be promoted, it was proposed only, that means should be adopted for previous enquiry and investigation. A Board of Commissioners, charged with the general subject, the precursor to the commencement of the grand Canals of New York, and the first measure of the Governments of New Jersey, of Ohio, of

Virginia, of Maryland, and of several other of the
States, in the mighty plans of their execution or
present undertaking, was recommended, alike from
precedent and the approval of experience in those
instances, and every where and at all times, must be
a prudent, if not necessary step, towards the devel-
opment of the capacities and resources of a country
for a system of public works of extensive and lasting importance. Much diversity of opinion is known
to prevail upon the preferable mode of facilitating
travel and transportation. *Canals* and *Railroads*
have each their respective advocates, while probably, the election of either, in most cases, must be
decided entirely by a regard to the face of the earth
over which their construction is proposed. What
method better calculated to resolve all questions
of this nature, than by a reference to men, experi-
mentally taught in mechanics, in hydraulics, in the
science of geology, the strata of the earth, the character of soils,—and skilled by observation and experience, in those calculations and deductions, by
which labour and expense may be correctly esti-
mated, and advantages and results, immediate and
prospective, satifactorily shown? It is not improb-
able that applications will continue to be addressed
to the Legislature to incorporate Canal and Rail-
way Companies, and for countenance and aid in the
objects of such associations. There are yet san-
guine and strenuous advocates for the construction
of a Canal from the Harbor of Boston, by a Northern route, to a point high upon the Connecticut

River, while the feasibility of a more Southern course than either of those examined by the late Commissioners, has been earnestly insisted on. A water communication from Norwich, in the State of Connecticut, by the Quinnabaug River to Brookfield, and thence in a Southerly direction, traversing the course of the Blackstone Canal, and by the waters of the Charles River to Boston, has been more recently proposed. A Ship channel between Barnstable Bay, and Buzzard's Bay, across the isthmus, and the connexion of Boston harbor with Narraganset Bay, by a canal through the Counties of Norfolk and Bristol, by the Weymouth and Taunton Rivers, as objects of national moment no less than of local concern, have engaged the favorable attention of the General Government, and in the distribution of the public bounty we might reasonably rely upon liberal contributions from the National Treasury to their accomplishment, whenever there shall be manifested the requisite spirit and confidence to engage in them. These and all projects of like kind, whether to be executed by public means or left to the labors of private enterprize, require leisure and deliberate investigation. It is no less the office of a wise Government to endeavor to secure from the waste of expenditure, upon visionary and fruitless schemes, the wealth of individuals, than to preserve the treasures of the State. To effect this, to guard adventurers from ruinous losses, and the community from discouraging and humiliating disappointments, all plans, which are proposed for

similar purposes, should be subjected to the same
test of examination, and their approval or rejection
should be the result of the application of an uni-
form standard of utility and profit, by which they
are compared. This will give consistency to a
system of improvement, which will exclude injurious conflicts of opinion and interest, and produce
the utmost advantage of a well directed appropriation of the public resources.

I cannot allow myself to pass from this topic without suggesting an additional consideration deserv-
ing of attention, when estimating the relative advantages of Canals and Railroads as measures of internal improvement, wherever the nature of the country will admit of the election. However, either, as
a mere mode of conveyance, may well subserve
this purpose of their construction, yet, the more
extended and beneficial influences of Canals in the
general improvement of Country, seem to me too
important and decisive to be lightly regarded. A
Railroad is a mere *passage way* for travel and
transportation. It has no other connexion or de-
pendence than upon intercommunication. Even if
it may facilitate this, at less expense, and in a
greater degree than a Canal, by being less liable
to interruption in its use, from accident, and weath-
er, and the frosts of winter, still, to some extent,
it is exposed to obstructions from the same causes,
while all the favourable differences may be coun-
terbalanced, by the greater convenience of passing
on Canals, and the superior adaptation of *Boats* to

3

Cars, for the accommodation of the infinite variety, in weight and bulk, of produce and products, which the pursuits, habits and occasions of this Country, through any considerable reach of population, will at different times, and often at the same time, present for carriage. Besides, Canals create new capacities and powers for artificial improvement.— From their reservoirs and feeders they may be caused to furnish increased and better regulated supplies of water for the use of manufactories and the convenient and profitable exercise of the mechanic arts. Their waters too, percolating their banks, irrigate and enrich the adjacent lands. Husbandry is thus invited to their cultivation. Along their courses, population, business, prosperity and wealth soon mark the progress of general improvement. Such has been the observation of the past, and is in the yet greater promise of future enterprise. Let not these remarks be regarded as entirely speculative. They are suggested by the opinions of skilful men, who have witnessed their practical illustration. Nor let me be understood as intending any discouragement to the construction of Railways, wherever situation, and the character of business, giving occasion to transportation, may warrant their adoption. It is important that there should be correct and definite opinions on these subjects. While uncertainty exists, and different modes of improvement, without distinction or discrimination in the circumstances of their application, find preferences with different minds, little will be attempted, and nothing successfully accomplished. To institute inquiries, which will give to the public conclusive and useful results, is worthy the attention of Government. The fitness and expediency of the measure, in relation to works of internal improvement in this Commonwealth, is renewedly and respectfully recommended to the consideration of the Legislature.

In compliance with a resolve of the Legislature of the 24th of February last, I early made the communication therein requested to the President of the United States upon the subject of the Resolutions of the Legislature of Maine, which had been transmitted for the consideration and concurrence of this Government, in relation to the public lands within the limits of that State and upon the north-eastern boundary of the United States, and to measures for ascertaining the monuments, and establishing the line of division between those lands and the British possessions. An answer to this communication, recently received from the Department of State, shows the earnest attention which has been given to the subject by the national Executive, and affords satisfactory assurance, that every competent step has been, and will continue to be taken to comply with the wishes, and to secure the rights of the States particularly interested. Copies of this correspondence will be submitted to you. The proposition in the *second* of the Resolutions of the Legislature of Maine, referred to in the letter of Mr. Clay, not having been acceded to by

this Commonwealth, no collision or controversy
with the British authorities need be apprehended
from the measures therein contemplated.

Since the adjournment of the last General Court,
His Excellency Governor Parris has transmitted
to me, expressly for the information of this government, a copy of an act of the Legislature of Maine,
passed on the 17th of February last, appropriating
four thousand dollars, on the part of that State, as
a contingent fund, for defraying the one half of
the expense of surveying the lands and for other
charges, exclusive of the personal compensation of
the Commissioners, as provided for in the act of
separation. In presenting this document to your
notice, I have to accompany it with a communication addressed to me by the Board of Commissioners, in reference to the execution of their duties, and containing an intelligent and earnest ex-
position of their views of advantage to the States,
from proceeding in the surveys and division of
the lands, the present season. After a careful attention to these representations, in connexion with
former communications on the same subject, and
from personal knowledge resulting from my en-
gagement heretofore in this commission, I cannot
but express the opinion, that provision should be
made for enabling the Commissioners to execute
their intended surveys. The act of separation
was, in itself, a compact between this Commonwealth and the people of Maine. It stipulated for
the division of the public lands within the period

of ten years, and pledged the faith of both governments to the appointment of Commissioners for
this purpose, and to defray, in moieties, the expense. Two-thirds of the limited period has already elapsed, and there remains much labor to be
performed in the completion of the work.—Neither State can enjoy their respective rights of property, until partition, and the assignment to them,
of their respective purparties. While the lands
remain in common, they cannot be settled, or sold.
For either party, therefore, to withold the means,
by the instrumentality of which only, the other can
receive the benefit and improvement of the property, may justly be complained of as an act of
wrong.—Any apprehensions which have been indulged, that the proposed surveys will involve us
in controversies with British subjects or officers
in the neighboring Province, and thus tend to embarrass the Government of the United States in
their negotiations to obtain a settlement of the
boundary line, are thought by the Commissioners
to be unfounded. The surveys will be under their
direction, and their recent communication contains
an explicit assurance, that no such consequences
will follow. Indeed, it appears from their representations, that the lines now to be run are *west*
and *north* of those traversed the last year, without interruption and without complaint, by the
British. Much confidence may justly be reposed
in the intelligence of these gentlemen, on this subject, and in the continued and satisfactory exer-

cise of that judgment and discretion for which they are eminently distinguished.

It has been objected that a more beneficial and less expensive partition of the lands might be made, by large divisions, and the assignment of certain designated portions to this Commonwealth, and the residue to Maine. It is sufficient to answer, that this business, by the express terms of the act of separation, is, *exclusively*, with the Commissioners, and that the government of neither State have any control over the mode of division, unless it be by negotiation and agreement between them. Besides, this commission is so peculiarly constituted, by an equal number of Representatives, as it were, of the interests of each State, that to guard against a possible prejudice or advantage to the one over the other, it has hitherto, in practice, been found necessary, upon every assignment, to make equal divisions of lands in the same situation and of like quality, and to determine the distribution of the parts by lot. From the very extent and character of this property, it must be obvious, that the interest of both parties is the same, in obtaining lands, which are most in the way of settlement, or are valuable for their timber, and will be first in demand in the market. Hence, no division has yet been made, which had not respect to the *equal value of equal quantities*, and the expectation of inducing to any other mode of assignment, under the commission, is utterly vain. It must therefore now rest with the Legislatiire of Massachusetts to decide, whether the stipulations in the act of separation shall be further executed. The responsibility of suspending them by one party, must be great; where the right to do so, is questionable, and the injury to the other party, certain. An appropriation rendered necessary to meet a balance of expenses incurred in the surveys of the last year, as well as to prosecute the objects of the commission, was recommended to the attention of the Legislature by special message, on the 13th of January last. To this document, with the papers which accompanied it, in explanation, on the files of the last session, I beg leave to refer you. The grant was prevented, at that time, by the disagreeing votes of the two houses. It has thus unfortunately happened, that orders drawn by the Commissioners in favor of persons, who, under their direction, have rendered services for the government, have not been satisfied. This circumstance will excuse the more earnestness in inviting your immediate consideration of the propriety of now making an appropriation corresponding with that, which has been certified, on the part of the State of Maine.

It cannot but afford to the Legislature the highest gratification to be informed, that the liberal and philanthropic provisions of the Government for the relief and instruction of the unhappy of our fellow beings who are deaf and dumb, have been carried into effect, as far as any occasion has presented. Although *every* applicant for this charity, within the description of the Resolves, has received a certificate of admission into the asylum at Hartford, there yet remains one vacancy. This circumstance affords the delightful hope, that the number of the unfortunate and dependent of this class of afflicted humanity is less considerable than had been apprehended. There are now forty-six pupils in the asylum, at the expense of this Commonwealth, and five other persons, in whose favour certificates have been granted, will probably be placed there immediately.

Copies of Resolutions, passed by the Legislatures of the States of Indiana and of Maine, respectively, disapproving of certain amendments to the constitution of the United States proposed by the General Assembly of the State of Tennessee, and copies of several resolutions of the Legislature of Louisiana approving of an amendment proposed by the Legislature of Georgia, and disapproving of an amendment proposed by the General Assembly of Ohio, have been officially transmitted to me to be laid before the Legislature of this Commonwealth. The subjects of all these Resolutions have heretofore been considered by the Legislature upon the original propositions of the States offering the amendments.

I have the unwelcome office of communicating the resignation, by the Honourable JAMES LLOYD, of his seat in the Senate of the United States, which he has so long filled with great distinction, and with eminent service to the State and the nation. His ability, valuable experience, fidelity and firmness, in the discharge of duty, are a loss to this Commonwealth in the Councils of the Union, which will awaken the utmost anxiety of the Legislature, to supply. Copies of his letter addressed to me, explanatory of the cause of his resignation, in the state of his health, and expressive of his senti-ments on the occasion, which I am requested to convey to you, I shall hasten to transmit.

It becomes also my duty to apprize you, that a vacancy exists in the office of Major General, of the *Sixth* Division of militia, occasioned by the re-signation and honorable discharge of Major Gen-eral Ivers Jewett.

I have great regret, that it is not in my power to inform you, that any provision has yet been made by the General Government for the settle-ment of the Massachusetts Claim. The Resolu-tions, expressing the sense of the Legislature upon the subject, at the last session, were promptly com-municated by me to each of the Senators and Rep-resentatives of this Commonwealth in Congress, and I have pleasure in offering you the assurance of their zealous efforts, with the cooperation and concert of the Delegation from the State of Maine, to bring the business to an immediate and satisfac-tory issue. The able discussions which were had on the floor of the House of Representatives, are believed to have produced a favourable impression. They cannot fail to do away much of misconcep-tion and long indulged prejudice, and prepare the

4

minds of those, who have hitherto resisted every approach to an investigation of the claim, hereafter, to consider it upon its merits. The Bill which had been reported in the House of Representatives by the military Committee, and was before a Committee of the whole House, promised to be the occasion of continued debate, and it was not thought useful to press the discussion, in the impatience and at the close of a protracted session of Congress. The opinions which are entertained by our Representatives, on the present state of the subject, have been expressed to me in a recent communication, copies of which, together with all the correspondence, subsequent to my last transmission of Documents to the Legislature, which has been had by me with the delegation through the attention of the Hon. Mr. Lloyd, the senior Senator from this Commonwealth, and who, in several meetings of the Delegates from both States, acted as their Chairman, will be laid before you. However, delays and disappointments may attend the prosecution of the rights of the State, those rights can never, with propriety, be abandoned. It is due alike to our interest and our honor, that this demand should be persisted in. The Claim of Massachusetts rests upon its own justice, and the obligation of the general government to provide for its payment. As a member of the Confederacy, we were, from the first and at all times, entitled to a favorable hearing from the Representatives of the nation; and whenever this measure of duty shall be fulfilled, towards us, we may confidently trust, that all objections to the allowance of the claim, founded in error and misapprehension, will be made to yield to the force of evidence and of argument, in its support.

The Delegations having expressed an opinion, upon the resignation of the late Agent, that "it would not be necessary that a new agent to proceed in auditing the accounts should attend at Washington during the session of Congress," none has been appointed. I have however, supposed, that the authority to make such appointment exists in the Executive, under the Resolves of the 12th of June 1824. Some inconsiderable expenses have been authorized and incurred for clerical services in the preparation of papers for the use of the delegation and in the care and preservation of the documents. The appropriation heretofore made for contingent charges appearing to have been exhausted, I recommend to the Legislature a further provision for this purpose ; and in view to the probable occasion for the future employment of an agent, agreeably to the suggestion of the Delegations, "whenever a Bill for the payment of the claim, in whole or in part, may be passed by Congress, or such other circumstances may occur as to make the appointment of such agent expedient." I also advise, to a revision of all the Resolves now in force, on that subject.

In turning our views from the peculiar interests of the Commonwealth, they rest with proud satisfaction upon the peace, prosperity, and glory of our

Country. With a few more days, a half century of
years will have completed their revolutions, since
that event, the boldest in the deeds of valor, the
noblest in the page of history, which, in proclaim-
ing the natural, equal and unalienable rights of
men, severed the dependant Provinces of America,
from the legitimacy of foreign dominion, and created them a free and sovereign nation. Well may
we now dwell with admiration and joy, on the
deep contrast of that fate-impending period with
the splendor and greatness of the present time.
Through the experience of nearly fifty years, in
peace and in war, amidst the conflicts of the elder
world and in the convulsions and overthrow of
mighty Kingdoms, this only Republic has stood
unshaken. With a fixed and settled written constitution of popular government, administered by a
succession of wise and patriotic Citizens, voluntarily called by the people to the public service, it
has attained to the highest elevation in the rank
of nations. In the full fruition of national independence, of the blessings of personal liberty, pro-
tection of property, the rights of conscience and of
private judgment, and in all the business, improvements, and refinements of Society, the People of
the United States are, at this moment, preeminently
happy, above all others of the earth. The pros-
pect of the future is unclouded, as has been the
brightest period of the past. How should these
considerations animate us with renewed gratitude
and devotion to the God of our Fathers, who in-

spired them with wisdom to erect this wondrous fabric of political Freedom, and gave them strength and constancy to maintain these goodly Institutions of Religion, and Learning, and Civil Government, until in their peaceful enjoyment, by the cultiva-, tion of patriotism, and knowledge, and virtue, they may be perpetuated in their posterity, to the end of time.

LEVI LINCOLN.

MESSAGE.

Gentlemen of the Senate, and
  Gentlemen of the House of Representatives :—

I transmit by the Secretary of the Commonwealth, copies of the several Documents referred to in the communication, which I had personally the honor to make to the two Houses of the Legislature, in Convention, this day. LEVI LINCOLN.
Council Chamber, June 6, 1826.

Documents relating to the North Eastern Bounda-
ry Line.

Governor Lincoln's letter to the President of the United States.

EXECUTIVE DEPARTMENT OF MASSACHUSETTS,
Worcester, Mass. March 10, 1826.
To His Excellency John Quincy Adams, President of the U. States.

SIR,—In compliance with a resolve of the Legislature of this Commonwealth, I have the honor to present to your notice and consideration, copies of sundry official papers, which relate to the subject of the line of division between the British possessions, and the public lands belonging to this Commonwealth and the State of Maine, within the territorial limits of the latter government, and upon the North Eastern Boundary of the United States.

From the anxiety which is felt upon this contro-
verted question of Boundary, and the manifest interest of the States of Massachusetts and Maine,
in the immediate sales and settlement of the lands,
the attention of the General Government is the.
more earnestly asked to the object expressed in
the accompanying resolutions; and in transmitting
them, in obedience to the will of the Legislature,
I beg permission respectfully to solicit the early
adoption of such measures as will most effectually
secure the right and interest of the States in whose
behalf I am honored with the opportunity of addressing you on this occasion.

With renewed assurances of the most respectful
and faithful consideration,

Your Obt. Svt.   LEVI LINCOLN.

To His Excellency Levi Lincoln.

DEPARTMENT OF STATE;

Washington, May 13, 1826.

SIR,—I am charged by the President with the
acknowledgment of his receipt of the letter addressed to him by your Excellency under date —
day of March last, and of the documents accompanying it, to all of which he has given attentive
and respectful consideration.

The question depending between Great Britain,
and the United States, respecting our North Eastern boundary, so interesting to the Common-

wealths of Massachusetts and Maine, has had much of the anxious attention of the Executive Government of the United States, and will continue to engage it until that question is brought to a satisfactory conclusion. Circumstances beyond our control, have prevented the resumption of the negociations relating to that and other subjects, which were suspended in the Summer of the year before the last, with an understanding between the parties that they were again to be renewed. Mr. Gallatin, lately appointed Envoy Extraordinary and Minister Plenipotentiary, to the Court of St. James, will be instructed to lose no time in reviving the negociations, and bringing them to an issue. In the mean time your Excellency has been already apprised by a letter which I had the honor of addressing to you on the 15th day of December 1825, that the President wishes that whatever steps may be taken by the Commonwealths of Massachusetts and Maine, should be in a spirit of moderation and forbearance, so as to avoid adding to the difficulties already not inconsiderable in the way of negotiation. If those Commonwealths should consider it necessary in conformity to the second resolution of the Legislature of Maine, adopted in January last, " to cause the Eastern and Northern lines of the State of Maine to be explored, and the monuments upon those lines mentioned in the Treaty of 1783, to be ascertained in such manner as may be deemed most expedient, the President hopes their proceedings will be guided by the same spir-

it. With respect to the documents and papers necessary to establish and illustrate' our title, the
two Commonwealths may rely upon the careful
preservation of those which are possessed in this
Department, and which are believed to be sufficient
to support it.

If in the progress of negociations, other eviden-
ces conducing to that object should. be wanted, it
ought to be procured at the expense of the Government of the United States.

I have the honor to be, with great respect,

Your Excellency's, most obt. humble serv't.

II. CLAY.

Documents relating to the Public Lands in Maine.

Governor Parris' letter.

STATE OF MAINE, EXECUTIVE DEPARTMENT,
Portland April 27, 1826.
SIR,—I have the honor to transmit, for the information of the Government of the State over which you preside, a copy of " an additional act, to provide for carrying into effect certain stipulations in the act for erecting the District of Maine into a separate' State; passed by our Legislature at its late session.

With assurance of, great respect,
I am, Sir, your obed't serv't,
ALBION K. PARRIS.
His Excellency Levi Lincoln,
Boston, Mass.

STATE OF MAINE.

In the year of our Lord one thousand eight hundred and twenty-six.

An additional Act to provide for carrying into effect certain stipulations in the act for erecting the District of Maine into a separate State.

BE it enacted by the Senate, and House of Representatives, in Legislature assembled, That for defraying the one half of the expense of surveying the lands in the State of Maine, surveyed, and to be surveyed and divided, the charges attending such surveys, and also for defraying one half of the compensation of the Secretary of the Board of Commissioners, and paying for the stationary necessary to be used by them, exclusive of the personal expenses of said Commissioners, the sum of four thousand dollars, be, and hereby is appropriated as a contingent fund, to be drawn for and paid as provided in the act to which this is additional.

In the House of Representatives, February 16, 1826.—This bill having had three several readings, passed to be enacted.

JOHN RUGGLES, *Speaker.*

In Senate, February 16, 1826.—This bill having had two several readings, passed to be enacted.

JONAS WHEELER, *President.*
February 17th, 1826.

Approved,
ALBION K. PARRIS.

STATE OF MAINE,
Secretary of State's Office, ⎱
March 31, 1826. ⎰

I hereby certify, that the foregoing is a true copy of the original deposited in this office.

Attest,
A. NICHOLS, *Secretary of State.*

Communication from the Commissioners to the Governor of Massachusetts.

The undersigned Commissioners, appointed by virtue of the Act for separating Maine from Massachusetts, having been informed that appropriations for making the survey of lands referred to in their Report made in January last, have not been made by the Legislature of Massachusetts, although such appropriations have been made by the Legislature of Maine, apprehending this will materially interrupt the execution of the important trust devolved upon them, and may essentially prejudice the interest of the two States in the property owned by them in common, feel it their duty, briefly to state the grounds upon which they have proceeded.

By the act of Separation, after providing that the public lands in Maine should be owned equally by both States, the authority and duty of the Commissioners are plainly and clearly declared, and among other things it is expressly stipulated that they should have authority to divide all the public lands in the State of Maine, in such way and manner as they should adjudge to be equal ; they are also authorized to cause such surveys to be made from time to time, as they should determine to be expedient : and the expense of such surveys and division is to be paid in equal shares, by the two States. The Commissioners are not only authorized but required to perform their duties, so that all the land in the District of Maine, owned by the Commonwealth before the separation, shall be divided within ten years from the filling up of the commission, and their acts and decisions are made final and conclusive, unless by the joint agreement of the Commonwealth and State, some other course be provided. No such agreement has, as yet, been made; the commission was filled up in 1820; a variety of causes, not necessary now to be detailed, has prevented as great progress in the division as might, perhaps, have been anticipated. Among others, the questions agitated about the boundaries of the State of Maine induced the Commissioners to pause for a time, in order to obtain information on the subject.

When the attention of the Commissioners was called to the subject of further divisions, by the Resolve of the Legislature of Massachusetts, passed in June last, they took pains to acquire information, and determined that two surveys should be made the past season, one of which was south of a line running west from the monument, and the other embraced two ranges of townships on the eastern boundary, extending north from the aforesaid line to the River St. John's, being a distance of nearly sixty miles.

These surveys were made the last year, and the land contained in them was divided. By the report and personal representation of the Surveyor, who went on the eastern line, Joseph Norris, Esq. in whom entire confidence may be placed, it appeared that he did not meet with any interruption, in making that, survey, from any quarter; and the Commissioners are not informed that this survey has been complained of by the British government or any of its agents.

By the reports of the Surveyors, as well as by other information, the land west and north of the surveys, made last season, is valuable, and generally suitable for settlement and cultivation, and likely to be settled whenever surveyed and offered for sale. The Commissioners, therefore, at their meeting at Portland, in December last, unanimously resolved, that it would be expedient to make surveys of five ranges of townships, making in the whole, sixty-five townships, and to take measures to effect it, during the ensuing season. Whatever may be the powers confided to the Commissioners, they are satisfied that whenever surveys are to be made, it is interesting to both States that funds should be at the disposal of the Board, to enable them to advance to the Surveyors, a sum equal to obtain the necessary out-fits for the survey. Among the reasons for ordering the contemplated survey the current year are the following:—the land proposed to be surveyed is generally of superior quality, much better than the remaining land in general; it is liable to constant intrusions and depredations from its contiguity to the waters of the St. John's, and to have settlements gradually made upon it, either actually under authority of the British government, or under pretence of it, and to be stript of its valuable timber ; it is contiguous to surveys made the last season on the east and ion the south, and can, this year, be better and more cheaply surveyed than at a future period. Having made t e survey, on the east of this land, last year, without interruption and, without complaint, there is no reason to apprehend that surveys, now to be made, will be interrupted or complained of. In discharge of the Commissioner's duty of dividing the land, a fair opportunity offers, without exciting uneasiness, of exercising an act of ownership which may be important to the interests of the States. The land west of this tract, by the survey, will be better known, and the mode of making further divisions can hereafter be better ascertained. If either of the States are disposed to sell or appropriate any of the land after it is divided, it can be done ; if either or both are disposed to retain it, the survey and divisions do not control the course to be adopted.

As to the land west of the proposed survey, it is doubtful whether it will be expedient to survey it into so small tracts as townships of six miles square. From some representations, the survey of part of it will be next to impossible. Satisfied from all accounts that British subjects are constantly making inroads on this territory, while they claim of us that nothing should be done to assert our claim, the Commissioners have not felt it their duty to abstain from surveying and dividing it.

To carry into effect the determination of the Board for a further survey, and with the object of saving the expense of a meeting of all the members, a committee was appointed to contract for the necessary surveys, who issued, and made public, a notice of the intended surveys, and invited those disposed to undertake the service, to make written proposals to them for doing it.

This Committee attended at the time and place appointed, and received proposals for making the survey, which was entirely satisfactory; but finding that no appropriations are made, and that the decision of the Board is not wholly satisfactory, they have declined proceeding.

Whenever the respective Legislatures shall provide the means of carrying into effect the terms of separation, the Commissioners are disposed to proceed, and to exercise their best discretion in discharging the duties devolved upon them by their appointment, and if no further services are required of them, they are content to be discharged.

March 6, 1826.

GEORGE BLISS,
CHARLES TURNER,
REUEL WILLIAMS,
SILAS HOLMAN,
BENJ. J. PORTER,
DANIEL ROSE,

To his Excellency Levi Lincoln, Esq.
Governor of the Commonwealth of
Massachusetts.

Documents relating to the proposed amendments to the Constitution of the United States.

EXECUTIVE DEPARTMENT,
Indianapolis, Indiana, Jan. 25, 1826.
In obedience to the enclosed Resolution, I have the honor herewith of transmitting to you a Joint Resolution of the General Assembly of the State of Indiana, disapproving of the amendment proposed to the constitution of the United States, by the State of Tennessee passed November 25th, 1825. Most respectfully your Obt. Svt.
J. BROWN RAY.
His Excellency the Governor of Massachusetts.

A JOINT RESOLUTION
Disapproving the amendment proposed by the State of Tennessee to the Constitution of the United States.
Resolved, By the General Assembly of the State of Indiana, That it is inexpedient to make the amendment to the Constitution of the United States, on the subject of electing President and Vice President of the United States as proposed in the Resolutions of the General Assembly of the State of

Tennessee, passed November 25, 1825, and that this General Assembly do hereby disapprove of the same.

Resolved, That this General Assembly do also disapprove of the amendment of the Constitution of the United States, as proposed by the Resolutions of the General Assembly of Tennessee aforesaid, providing that no Member of Congress shall be eligible to any office within the gift or nomination of the President of the United States, during the period for which he shall have been elected, and for six months thereafter, except appointments in the regular Army or Navy of the United States.

Resolved, That His Excellency the Governor, be, and he is hereby requested to transmit a copy of the foregoing resolutions to the Governors of the different States, and to each of our Senators and Representatives in Congress.

ROBERT M. EVANS,

Speaker of the House of Representatives.

JOHN II. THOMPSON,

President of the Senate.

Approved, January 20, 1826.

J. BROWN RAY.

———

STATE OF LOUISIANA.

EXECUTIVE DEPARTMENT,

New-Orleans, Feb. 1, 1826.

SIR,—I have the honor to transmit you herewith,

a copy of a 'Resolution, passed by the Legislature of this State, and to request that you will lay the same before the Legislature of the State over which you preside.

I have the honor to be, very respectfully,

Your Excellency's Obt. Svt.

H. JOHNSON.

To His Excellency the Governor of the State of Massachusetts.

RESOLUTION

Relating to an amendment proposed by the State of Georgia, to the Constitution of the United States.

Resolved, By the Senate and House of Representatives of the State of Louisiana, in General Assembly convened, that they do concur in the amendment proposed by the State of Georgia to the Constitution of the United States, passed the 22d day of December, 1823, in the words following, to wit:

"That no part of the Constitution of the United States ought to be construed, or shall be construed, to authorise the importation or ingress of any persons of color, into any one of the United States, contrary to the laws of such State."

Resolved, That the Governor of this State be and he is hereby requested to communicate this Resolution to the Executive of the different States, and request that the same may be submitted to their respective Legislatures.

A. B. ROMAN,
    Speaker of the House of Representatives.
H. S. THIBODAUX,
                President of the Senate.
Approved,—30th January, 1826.

H. JOHNSON,
Governor of the State of Louisiana.

———

EXECUTIVE DEPARTMENT,
New Orleans, Feb. 16, 1826.

SIR,—In compliance with the request of the Legislature of this State, I have the honor to transmit to you a copy of a resolution of the said Legislature, passed at their present session, and to request that you will be pleased to lay the same before the Legislature of the State over which you preside.

I am, with great respect,
    Your Excellency's Obt. Svt.
                H. JOHNSON.

His Excellency the Governor of the State of Massachusetts.

———

RESOLUTION.

Resolved, By the Senate and House of Representatives of the State of Louisiana in General Assembly convened, That this Legislature does not 'concur. in certain resolutions adopted by the General Assembly of Ohio, at their session in the year one thousand eight hundred and twenty-four, proposing a plan for the gradual emancipation of Slaves, and that the Governor be requested to transmit a copy of this resolution to the Executive of each of the United States.

A. B. ROMAN,
Speaker of the House of Representatives.
H. S. THIBODAUX,
President of the Senate.

Approved, Feb. 16, 1826.

H. JOHNSON,
Governor of the State of Louisiana.

STATE OF MAINE.

EXECUTIVE DEPARTMENT,
Portland, Feb. 20, 1826.

SIR,—In compliance with the request contained in the enclosed Resolution of the Legislature of Maine, I transmit a copy thereof to be laid before the Legislature of the State over which you preside.

With high consideration, I am, Sir,
Your Obt. Svt.
ALBION K. PARRIS.

His Excellency the Governor of Massachusetts, Boston.

STATE OF MAINE.

Resolve against the amendment to the Constitution proposed by Tennessee.

Resolved, That the amendment to the Constitution of the United States proposed by the General Assembly of the State of Tennessee on the twenty-fifth of November last, and forwarded to the Governor of Maine, is not approved by the Legislature of this State. And the Governor is requested to transmit a Copy of this Resolve to the Executive of each of the United States.

In House of Representatives, Feb. 14, 1826.—Read and passed.

JOHN RUGGLES, Speaker.

In Senate, Feb. 16, 1826.—Read and passed.

JONAS WHEELER, President.

Feb. 17, 1826.—Approved,

ALBION K. PARRIS.

———

STATE OF MAINE.

SECRETARY OF STATE'S OFFICE,
Portland, Feb. 20, 1826.

I hereby certify that the foregoing is a true Copy of the original deposited in this Office.

Attest,   A. NICHOLS,
Secr'y of State.

Washington, Feb. 11, 1826.

SIR,—I have the honor to transmit to you herewith, the proceedings of the adjourned meeting of
the Delegations of Massachusetts and Maine, holden this day in reference to the claim on the General Government for the services of the militia during the late war; together with the copy of a note
from Mr. Sullivan on that subject.

  With sentiments of great respect, t.

     I have the honor to be,

      Your Obt. humble Svt.

       JAMES LLOYD.

His Excellency Governor Lincoln.

Friday, Feb. 11.

At an adjourned meeting of the Delegations from
 Massachusetts and Maine in reference to the
 Claim for Militia services,

  The Bill reported to the House of Representatives was called for and read; when the Committee appointed at the last meeting, to ascertain from
the War Department, and from Mr. Sullivan, the
amount which would be provided for by the Bill
now pending before the House of Representatives
reported, that they had seen the Secretary of War

and the third Auditor, both of whom declined giving any specific information on the subject; and that they had also applied to Mr. Sullivan, from whom an answer in writing had been received (which is herewith transmitted) whereupon

Resolved, That a Committee of three, consisting of Mr. Davis, Mr. Bailey, and Mr. Lincoln, be appointed to examine the reports which have been made on the subject of the Massachusetts Claim, and to report the amount they may consider, as embraced by it, at an adjourned meeting of the Delegations to be called by the Committee, as soon as they are ready to report.

Resolved, That it be recommended, that the phraseology of the last proviso be so proposed to be amended, as to read, " where the troops employed, were not specifically and *unreasonably* withheld," &c.

The Delegations then adjourned to meet when notified by the Committee.

J. LLOYD, *Chairman.*

COPY.

Washington, 7th Feb. 1826.

To the Honorable Mr. Mills, and
Honorable Mr. Lincoln.

GENTLEMEN,—In compliance with your request, I have the pleasure to specify the portions of the claim, which are excluded from allowance by the latter clause of the second provision of the bill;

the first clause of this provision, which excludes all
services that were at variance with the views of
the General Government, has no bearing whatever
on our claim; none of our services being at variance with the views of the General Government,
if these views were the defence of the State.

The Claim for the South Boston service, reported by the 3d Auditor, as the 9th Division, amounts
to $165,672 64

That for a portion of the 12th and
13th Divisions, viz. Ryerson's Regi-
ment at Portland,   25,305 63

That for a portion of the 11th and
8th Divisions, viz. Sweet's Regiment
and Sherwin's Regiment and 2 Com-
panies of Artillery   25,504 39

To which may be added some con-
tingencies incident to these services,
say,   14,000 00
                                                     _____
                                                     $230,482 66
                                                     ════════════

It was impossible for the 3d Auditor to fix the
times, places, and occasions of these services, and
not perceive and present in his reports the facts
which bring these portions within the discriminat-
ing provision.

The reasons why the troops, who performed the
services, were withheld from the command of the
United States officers, can be explained in every
instance, in a manner to vindicate the State from
all imputation of design to embarrass the National

7

Government in its extremity, and all charge of dis-
loyalty to the Union; but in respect to the State's
right to reimbursement, the necessity of the services in defence of the soil is conclusive against all
objections.

The reasons, however, which withheld the troops,
may be useful in debate; and I shall be gratified
in the opportunity of communicating them, whenever you may desire; this may be done with the
most convenience and utility in personal inter-
views; but in whatever mode the Delegates may
honor me with inquiries, I shall consider it my duty to answer them at all times, and wherever I may
be, with promptitude, as I certainly shall with great
pleasure.

Respectfully, your Obt. Svt.
Signed, GEO. SULLIVAN.

Governor Lincoln's letter to Mr. Lloyd.

BOSTON, FEBRUARY 13, 1826.

To the Hon. James Lloyd.

SIR,—Your letters of the 1st and 3d instant,
with the several papers accompanying the latter,
were received in due course of the Mails, and I
now have the honor to express my particular
gratification in the very prompt and satisfactory regard which has been paid to my former communication, of which they are the evidence. These
papers have been transmitted by me to the Legis-

lature, and I trust I shall be enabled, in a few days, to forward to you an official expression of their opinion upon the subject to which they refer. In the mean time I hope to be permitted to rely upon the continued attention of yourself, and your honorable Colleague; with that of the Representatives in Congress, from this State, in inviting the co-operation of the Senators and Representatives from Maine, and in united and effectual measures to obtain a just and immediate provision, for the allowance and payment of the Claim. From the better opportunities, at Washington, for judging what the character of these measures should be, I have great pleasure and confidence in submitting them to the direction of the Delegations. Should any clerical services be required, at the expense of the State, you will please to consider yourself, in your discretion, fully authorized to command them.

I have the honor to be Sir, very truly
with entire respect,
Your Obt. Svt.   LEVI LINCOLN.

Copy of Resolutions of the Legislature with the Governor's Letter to the Delegates in Congress.

Commonwealth of Massachusetts.

In the year of our Lord, one thousand eight hundred and twenty six.

Resolved, That this Legislature concurs in the sentiments expressed by His Excellency the Gov-

ernor, in his Message respecting the Massachusetts Claim; and feels the greatest confidence that
he will exercise the powers heretofore delegated
to him by the Legislature, on the subject, so as
best to protect the rights and maintain the dignity
of this Commonwealth.

Resolved, That the present state of the Massachusetts Claim, requires the immediate attention of
the Senators and Representatives of this Commonwealth, in Congress, and that His Excellency
the Governor be requested to communicate this
opinion of the Legislature, in such manner as he
shall judge best.

House of Representatives February 7, 1826.—
Sent up for concurrence.

    TIMOTHY FULLER, *Speaker.*

In Senate, February 21, 1826.—Read and con-
curred.   NATH'L SILSBEE, *President.*

A true copy, Attest,

    EDWARD D. BANGS, *Secretary.*

—————

     Executive Department of Massachusetts, }
       February 21, 1826.   }

In compliance with the concurrent request of the
two branches of the Legislature of this Commonwealth, contained in the latter of the accompanying
Resolutions, I communicate, herewith, the expression of their opinions and wishes, in reference to
the "Massachusetts Claim," now pending before
Congress; and I add the assurance of my continued and most earnest desire, that the subject may

receive that prompt and effectual attention, which, in the opinion of the Delegations, from Massachusetts and Maine, shall best tend to secure a just, liberal, and honorable provision, for the allowance and payment of the debt. Printed, copies of the document referred to, in the first of the Resolutions, have been, heretofore, forwarded.

LEVI LINCOLN.

Mr. Lloyd's letter to Governor Lincoln.

Washington, Feb. 23, 1826.

SIR,—I had the honor to receive in course your Excellency's letter of the 13th inst. which I have not before acknowledged, under an expectation of being able to communicate the proceedings of the Delegations on the report of the Committee which was appointed at their last meeting, to ascertain as near as may be the amount which would be embraced by the Bill heretofore referred to and reported by the Military Committee of the House of Representatives.

That meeting has been holden this day.

Present,

The Senators from Massachusetts.

Gen. Chandler from Maine.

OF THE HOUSE OF REPRESENTATIVES:

From Massachusetts,	From Maine,
Mr. Allen	*Mr. Lincoln*
Mr. Bayley	*Mr. Anderson*
Mr. Crowninshield	*Mr. Burleigh*
Mr. Davis	*Mr. Herrick.*

Mr. Dwight	*Mr. Kidder*
Mr. Everett	*Mr. O'Brian*
Mr. Lock	*Mr. Sprague.*
Mr. Reed	
Mr. Varnum	

The letter of Governor Lincoln, of Feb. 13, having been read, the Committee appointed at the last meeting made a report in writing; when, after discussion, it was

Resolved, That the report be recommitted to the Committee reporting it, for the use of the Delegations in the House of Representatives in the discussion of the claim; who are authorized and requested to prosecute the claim, as efficiently and speedily as may be practicable; and to propose such amendments to the bill as at this time, or in its progress, they may deem expedient; and that the Chairman of the Committee be requested, at the expense of the State of Msssachusetts, to obtain a copy of the report to be transmitted to the Executive of the State, and five other copies for the use of the Delegations.

The meeting was then adjourned to convene at such time hereafter, should it be necessary, as may be designated by the members of the House of Representatives.

The report before alluded to shall be forwarded as soon as the copy is received.

Having the honor to be, Sir,
With great respect,
Your Obt. Svt.
JAMES LLOYD.
His Excellency Governor Lincoln.

Governor Lincoln's letter to Mr Lloyd.

EXECUTIVE DEPARTMENT, MASS.
Boston, Feb. 28, 1826.

To the Hon. James Lloyd,

SIR,—I have pleasure in acknowledging the receipt of your letter of the 23d inst.—The proceedings of the Delegations from Massachusetts and Maine, as they have been obligingly communicated by you, from time to time, cannot but meet the entire approbation of this government.

Your unintermitting and earnest endeavors to bring to a final and satisfactory result the claim of Massachusetts upon the General Government are particularly appreciated by myself—and I have great confidence, that the united efforts of the Delegates from the States particularly interested in this embarrassed, but very important subject, will be effectual to the maintenance of the honor, and just constitutional rights of the people and government of this ancient Commonwealth.

To preclude any *misapprehension,* or *misrepresentation,* which may be attempted, I take leave to trouble you with a copy of a letter addressed by me to Mr. Sullivan, *before* his discharge from his agency, of which you will please to make such use as occasion may require.

The Legislature of this Commonwealth will probably adjourn in the course of the present week. Any communications, therefore, with which I may be honored, after the receipt of this letter, will soonest reach me by being directed to Worcester.

I have the honor ever to be, Sir, with sentiments of entire respect, your Obedient Servant,

LEVI LINCOLN.

Extract from a letter of Hon. Mr. Lloyd, transmitting a Report of the Committee of the Delegations, March, 1826.

WASHINGTON, MARCH 3, 1826.

DEAR SIR,—Enclosed I transmit to you a copy of the Report of the Committee of the Delegations in Congress from Massachusetts, and Maine, in reference to the Claim for militia services, which I mentioned in my last: five other copies have been made out, which are now in the hands of the members of the House of Representatives.

With great respect, I am dear Sir, Your Obt. Svt.

J. LLOYD.

His Excellency Governor Lincoln.

———

The Committee appointed by the Delegations of Massachusetts and Maine, to ascertain as far as practicable the amount of the Claim of Massachusetts for militia services during the late war, which will be embraced and allowed, should the bill reported to the House of Representatives be passed into a law in its present form, ask leave to report as follows:

The Committee have examined the bill and consider its provisions as objectionable, both because the limiting provisos place the claim on a more unfavorable footing than those of other States, and because those provisos are ambiguous and difficult to interpret. It being, however, obvious to the Committee, that the bill proposes the adoption of a

- measure not likely to be favored by Congress, they have thought it advisable to look at all the provisions, and to compare them with the evidence by which the claim is supported, with a view to ascertain if any thing would probably be allowed, and if so, how much. It is not to be disguised, that this was a task of difficulty, and after all, has not led to any very conclusive results. The reasons are twofold; first, the provisions of the bill are not sufficiently definite: secondly, the evidence reported, which purports to be an abstract only of the proofs, is not sufficiently clear and certain, as to some important items of charge, to enable the Committee to determine in a satisfactory manner, whether those items are brought within the provisions of the bill or not.

The Committee have no hesitation in saying that a better bill is desirable ; but as an attempt to vary the provisions of the one reported, may endanger, and in the judgment of some of the Committee, defeat the claim, or rather the allowance of any portion of it at present; they will briefly state to the Delegations the opinions they have adopted, as to the operation of the bill, and the reasons for those opinions.

The bill in the first place authorizes and directs the Department of War to audit and settle under the *usual rules* in such cases, the claims of the State for militia services during the late war. The only inquiry as to this provision which seems important is, as to what is meant by *usual rules* ;

and it seems plain to the Committee that this expression has reference only to the items of charge,
and not to the character of the services performed,
or to the circumstances under which they were performed, for the bill proceeds immediately to establish rules as to these points of difficulty. The term
'usual rules' requires therefore the Department to
see that no other than such items of charge as have
been allowed to other States, shall be allowed to
Massachusetts, supposing the services rendered to
be unobjectionable. The bill next provides for the
allowance of two classes of claims; first in all cases
where the militia of the State were called out in
conformity with a *desire* or *requisition* of an officer
of the General Government; secondly, in all cases
where they were called out to repel actual invasion,
or under a well founded apprehension of invasion.
This second provision would undoubtedly embrace
and cover the claim, if it were not for the limiting
clauses which follow. It becomes, therefore, important to ascertain the true meaning of these clauses, as on them in a great measure is to depend the
present fate of the claim, if this bill should pass un-
altered. The first of these restraining clauses
which it is important to consider, forbids an allowance, provided the services of the militia for which
compensation is asked, were at variance with the
views of the General Government. The Committee are of opinion that this provision, presents no
obstacle to the allowance of the whole claim, for

there is no proof that the services were adverse to the views of the General Government. On the contrary the proof is strong, if not conclusive, that the *services* were imperatively necessary, and were render either to repel actual invasion of the territory of the United States, or to protect points in imminent danger of invasion. The provision makes no objection to the *authority* by which the troops were called out, or to the persons by whom they were commanded, but merely required that the *service* performed should not be at variance with the views of the General Government. The services were rendered in defence of the United States; the troops did, and performed, what it was the duty and wish of the United States to do, and therefore the services could not be at *variance* with the views of that Government.

The next and last limiting clause forbids allowance in all cases where the troops employed in the service were *specifically* withheld from the command of an officer or officers of the General Government *applying* for the same. This is the most objectionable feature of the bill, as it is not easy to forsee what will be held by the Department of War to be evidence of an *application* by an officer or officers of the General Government for the troops, or for the command of the troops; nor is it easy to foresee what will be deemed evidence of withholding specifically the troops, or the command of the troops upon such application. In considering this point, the Committee have been led to inquire, whether if a *requisition* for troops was made upon the Governor to defend certain points of exposure, and the Governor instead of complying with that *requisition*, at or about the same time called into the service under *his own* authority, troops to defend the same points, the requisition itself would, under such circumstances, be considered an *application* for the troops so called into the service, or for the command of them, within the meaning of this bill, and whether *neglecting* to deliver such troops to an officer of the United States, is to be considered as evidence of withholding them specifically.

If such a requisition by an officer of the U. States, is to be deemed evidence of applying for the command of troops called into service by the *authority of the State*, and if neglecting on the part of the Governor to place these troops under the command of a U. States officer, is to be taken as proof of withholding the command specifically, then will this limiting provision of the bill affect most deeply the claim, for it appears by the documents that General Dearborn, of the United States army, on the fifth of September 1814, made a *requisition* upon the Governor for 4,650 troops to be stationed as follows: 2,200 for the defence of Boston, 1,100 for Portland, 1,100 for Kennebunk, and 250 for York. It appears also that the Governor on the 6th of the same month issued an order independent of this *requisition*, bringing into the service for the defence of Boston, 3,728 troops, under the command of an officer of militia: about the same period, large bod-

ies of troops were called by state authority to. defend Portland, Kennebeck, and York: the same or
nearly the same points which General Dearborn
required the 4,650 troops to defend.' The requisition by General Dearborn and the detachments, by
the Governor were nearly simultaneous; a portion
of the troops being ordered out a day or two before, and the residue soon after. If this requisition
of General Dearborn can be considered as an application according to the terms of the bill, for the
command of these troops, or for the troops themselves, and the retention of the command in state
officers can be considered a denial of that application, then it would seem to follow, that all the troops
called out to defend the points designated in, the *requisition* were withheld, and nearly the whole of
the claim must be rejected. But the Committee
are not satisfied that in fairness, such a construction can be given to the bill. The language is this;
in cases when the troops employed in the same
(that is, the same services) were not withheld specifically from the command of an Officer of the
General Government applying for the same. The
word 'specifically' as here used would seem to im-
ply that there must be a plain, obvious and une-
quivocal withholding, and a withholding, of the
troops or the command of the troops *employed in
the service* from an officer of the United States, *applying* for the same. The Committee think moreover that the troops called into the service cannot
be identified with those demanded by the requisi-

tion. The proof of this is clear for they were called out by the order of the Governor without any reference to the requisition. Neither the numbers, nor the grade corresponded to the requisition; moreover, the Governor, on the 7th of September, the day following that on which his order was issued, distinctly informed the Secretary of War, that sometime previous, he had complied with a requisition of General Dearborn; but such inconveniencies had arisen, that the measure could not be repeated; and enclosed to the Secretary the order he had issued the day preceding. These facts shew that the troops were called into service by authority of the State and not by virtue of the requisition; and so the Third Auditor seems to consider it. The requisition therefore remained in the hands of the Governor wholly disregarded and unexecuted; and the troops that came into the service, came there by another authority, and for no purpose can be considered as the same demanded by the *requisition.* Hence the requisition seems to have no application to those troops, and is no proof of a demand either for the troops, or for the command of them; and if there was no demand, there can be no specific withholding of the command or of the troops. As the laws stood in 1814, the United States had the power of calling out the militia either by a direct order to the officers, or by a requisition upon the Governor, and if the latter method was adopted, an officer of the United States had no right to the command, until the troops were detached, and

brought to the place of rendezvous. The Bill with
its restraining provisions seems to be framed with a
view to meet the law as it existed :: for there would
seem to be but two cases in which the command
of the troops could be withheld specifically. If
for example, a requisition had been made upon the
Governor, and he had proceeded to comply with it,
by causing the troops required to be detached pur-
suant to the requisition, and marched to the place
of rendezvous, and then refused to deliver up the
command, it would be a specific withholding, such
as is contemplated by the bill. So also if troops
were found in service under the authority of the
State, and while so in service, a legal order should
be issued by a competent officer of the United
States, requiring them to enter into the service of
the United States, and the State authorities should
interpose, and prevent a transfer of the command,
it would also be a specific withholding, such as is
contemplated by the bill. But the troops in question were neither ordered out by the United States,
nor detached in compliance with a *requisition*, but
were brought into service by virtue of the State
Government, in the exercise of its own power. It
would seem therefore, that the requisition of
General Dearborn, cannot be considered either as
proof of an *application* for these troops, or for the
command of them.
It now only remains to be considered whether
there was any application made for the command
of these troops by an officer of the United States,

while they were in the actual service of the State. The Committee have examined the evidence as contained in the documents, to see if there was any thing touching this point, and they find but three important items of charge against which any objection of this kind can be urged. The first item we shall notice is contained in the charges for services under the head of Eleventh and Eighth Divisions, and is for the pay, &c. of a regiment commanded by Lieut. Col. Sweet, and another commanded by Lieut. Col. Sherwin, amounting to 25,339 dollars. The documents show, that propositions were made for placing these troops in the United States service, and that General Dearborn consented to receive them into that service, on their being organized into two Battalions instead of two Regiments; this, however, was not done, and the troops remained in State service. If these facts can be considered as furnishing proof of an application on the part of an officer of the United States for the command of the troops, the Committee consider that demand void, because a condition was annexed to it, by which the two regiments were to be reduced to Battalions, a portion of the officers to be dismissed, and the whole troops to be organized in a manner different from that required by law. Believing, as the Committee do, that the Bill intends a demand or application, which the State authorities were bound to obey, they do not consider these transactions as excluding this item from allowance. The next item to which the

Committee invite the attention of the Delegates is contained under the head of Twelfth and Thirteenth Divisions, and in the documents is denominated Lieut. Col. Ryerson's detached regiment. It appears by the third Auditors abstract of evidence that a larger body of troops were in service at and near Portland, under the command of Major General Richardson and that he, Col. Sumner, the agent of the State for defensive measures, and the Committee of safety for Portland had consultation with General Chandler of the United States army then commanding at that place; as to the force necessary for the defence of Portland; and it was decided that 1,100 men should be detached and placed in the service of the United States service, an order was accordingly issued, the detachment made; Col. Ryerson assigned to the command, and the residue of the troops dismissed. But some of the officers objected to being mustered into the United States service; and Ryerson being found fit for fatigue duty only, it was deemed most wise in the absence of General Chandler, who had gone to Portsmouth, to request General Richardson to remain in command; and he did so remain. The amount claimed for the services &c. of this detachment as we learn from Mr. Sullivan's letter is about $ 25,000. The substance of the evidence as it is gathered from the abstract of the Third Auditor, which is not very satisfactory seems to be this; a body of troops under a Major General was in service under State authority. The officers of the State then commanding proposed to a U. S. officer to place under his command a portion of these troops, and to dismiss the residue. The United States officer assented to it, and owing to the obstacles which have been mentioned, the arrangement was not carried into effect. The question is, whether the assenting to this arrangement, and agreeing to take into the service of the United States these troops, upon the *application* of the *State authorities,* is evidence of an *application* for the Command of the troops by an officer of the *United States,* and whether a failure on the part of the State officers to fulfil this engagement is to be held a denial of that application; and the Committee are not prepared to say it is one or the other. If it be an application for the command, it is made so by *construction,* and it is not specific, if by specific is meant direct and unequivocal. The United States did not apply at all, but *consented* on the *application* of the State *officers* to take the troops into the service. It was not, so far as we can learn, the intention of the United States officer to exert any power or authority vested in him on this occasion, he did not mean to order any portion of the militia under General Richardson into the United States' service under the law of '95, but merely to receive the troops if they were offered for his command; the Committee therefore repeat, that the demand or application contemplated by the bill must be such as is authorized by law; otherwise disregarding it, is no withholding of the command, or the troops. If, however, there are any doubts as to the effect of these transactions, it is believed, if the amendment proposed by inserting the word *unreasonably* after the word *specifically* should prevail, it must draw after it this item.

The last item of considerable magnitude which may be effected by transactions after the service commenced, is that audited under the 9th division, and is the claim for services rendered in the vicinity of Boston. On the 7th of September, the day after the order for calling for these troops was issued, the Governor gave notice to the Secretary of War of his measures, and inquired whether the troops would be paid by the United States. In answer to this communication, the Secretary, under date of September 17th, replies, and among other things says, " if the force which has been put into service by your Excellency has been required by Major General Dearborn, or received by him, and put under his command, that the expense attending it will be defrayed by the United States. It follows likewise as a necessary consequence, that if this force has been called into service by the authority of the State, independently of Major General Dearborn, and be not placed under him as commander of the district, that the State of Massachusetts is chargeable with the expense, and not the United States." The question with the Committee was, whether this reply is to be considered a requisition upon the Executive of Massachusetts by an officer of the United States to place these troops

under the command of General Dearborn, and
whether the neglect of the Executive to do it is a
refusal to place the troops in the service of the
United States. The question discussed is as to
the reimbursement of the expenses. The state-
ments of the Secretary are hypothetical, and not
directory; and there is much reason for believing
that the letter was never intended as an order of
the Executive of Massachusetts to place these
troops under General Dearborn. The whole authority of the United States, it seems by the letter
of the Secretary, was reposed in General Dearborn as to calling out the militia within his district,
and it seems pretty obvious, that the Secretary
did not intend to interfere with this authority, but
to leave it in his hands to be exercised according to his discretion. He did not mean, by his
letter to the Governor, to compel General Dearborn to receive these troops into the service, if in
his judgment they were not necessary, but merely
to say if in the end it was found that they acted
under the orders of General Dearborn, the expenses would be paid. If this is a correct view of the
subject, there is no impediment to the allowance
of this item, for the documents do not shew any
other requisition upon the Executive, or any other
officer, to place these troops under an officer of
the United States. The amount of this item is
165,000 dollars, according to Mr. Sullivan's state-
ment; and upon these facts it is for the delegations to judge, whether an amendment is necessary
to embrace it. The Committee have now gone

through with all the items sufficiently important to require an examination upon this occasion; and although they do not fully agree as to what may be considered as proof of a *specific* withholding of the troops, or the command of the troops, yet they concur in believing that the amount of claims to the allowance of which, objections may be made under this bill, does not exceed 200,000 dollars; they ought, however; to observe, that they ascertain the sums from Mr. Sullivan's letter, and not from any documents in print, as there are none that shew them.

The Committee would also observe that this examination of the character of the bill, and the evidence as applicable to it, has been entered into from an apprehension, that no bill can be passed without being shielded in a coat of mail through which it will be difficult to thrust a claim. They have taken it for granted, that whatever amendment may be offered, still no bill will pass without these outworks; and it is deemed an object to have them left in such a form, as that we may pass them, and find our way to the Treasury. They cannot, however, undertake to give any assurance; that a law would receive, in the War Department, the same construction which is here given it, as much will necessarily depend on the disposition and feelings with which the subject will be there met and examined. The Committee, in conclusion, have only to observe, that they beg pardon of the Delegations for asking their attention for so long a time to such a dry and unentertaining investigation.

Copy of a Letter from Gov. Lincoln to the Hon. James Lloyd.

.WORCESTER, MASS. MARCH 11, 1826.

To the Honorable James Lloyd,

SIR,—My return to the Country upon the prorogation of the Legislature, has delayed my receipt of your recent communication upon the subject of the Claim, which reached me only the last evening, by the way of Boston.

, I have perused with deliberate attention the Report of the Committee of the Delegations from Massachusetts and Maine, and see in it much of ability and ingenuity, yet it but adds to the regret at first experienced, on observing the *proviso*, in the bill reported by the Military Committee, as it confirms the apprehensions then entertained of its probable tendency and ultimate effect. It is manifestly objectionable both as an injurious assumption of the character of a portion of the services, hereafter to be discussed in the Department, and as creating an invidious distinction and discrimination between the claims of this Commonwealth, and those of other States, which have been provided for under a general appropriation, without this distinguishing and offensive suggestion of hostility to the General Government. Whether any portion of the services will be found, in fact, to fall within either branch of the *proviso*, is probably not expected to be matter of particular investigation before Congress. I have, therefore, rather regarded the introduction of the proviso into the Bill, as a gra-

tuitous caution against a favorable regard to the
whole subject, for it is entirely obvious, that if no
portion of the services are exposed to its application, it is unnecessary, and if they are of a description, which are constitutionally excluded from consideration, it needed not this rule to secure their
rejection. I have, however, great pleasure on this
occasion, in repeating the assurance of the most
entire satisfaction, which I personally feel, and
which I believe will be expressed by every enlightened man, in the course which has been pursued by the Delegations. It is indeed an object of
most anxious desire, that the claim should be
brought to an issue with the General Government,
and that now, after a delay of eleven years, from the
completion of the account, it should come distinctly to be known, upon what reasons it is, that justice can longer be postponed. It does not com-
port with the sovereignty of the State, to be sup-
plicating before the confederacy for that impartial
regard to its rights which was intended to have
been secured to each party to the compact. If it
will ever be proper to make provision for our demand, it may as well be done at once, as at any
subsequent period. Time is adding nothing to the
possession of facts on the subject. The minds of
men are, as unprejudiced now, as they will hereafter be ome. With most of the present members of
Congress, the events of the War, and the measures
which grew out of it, in this part of the country,
are rather matter of history or testimony by oth-

ers, than of personal observation and knowledge. The times are politically tranquil, and as it would seem, favorable for the exercise of judgment, unaffected by passionate recollections. Indeed, Sir, every consideration urges to the conclusion of this vexed and troubled question with the United States. The State is in want of the money, the honor of its Government is involved in the settlement of the claim,-and the confidence of the people, in the good faith of the Nation, will be greatly impaired by its longer denial.

You will please not to understand me, by these observations as wishing to precipitate the measures, which the prudence and judgment of the Delegations, far better advised than myself, may suggest. The subject is respectfully and with entire confidence submitted to their direction. It is only my intention, to communicate what I humbly apprehend to be the universal feeling here, that as soon as may be, the subject should be definitely disposed of, that it may no further tend to personal or political excitements, nor be the occasion of protracted trouble and accumulated expense, and of often disappointed expectations of justice.

Ever obliged by your communications, I am Sir, with sentiments of entire respect,

Your Obt. Svt.   LEVI LINCOLN.

Communication from the Delegates to Governor Lincoln.

Washington, May 8, 1826.

DEAR SIR,—We have thought you might wish to hear from some of us respecting the present situation of the claim. You are aware that it came on for consideration some weeks ago, and underwent a discussion of some 'length in the House. No vote was taken; but we think we may venture to say, that on the whole, the impression produced by the examination of the claim is favorable to its future allowance, in whole or in part. No doubt much of misapprehension has existed on this subject. The facts have been greatly misunderstood and the principles applicable to the occasion not adverted to, or not always sufficiently understood. To remove prejudices and misapprehension of this sort when extensively existing, is necessarily a work of time. We trust that something has been done towards this end, and having full confidence in the strength and justice of the grounds on which the claim rests, we entertain a confident expectation of its future adjustment and payment.

We are, Sir, with much regard,

Your Obt. Servts.

Samuel Lathrop	*B. W. Crowninshield*
Samuel C. Allen	*John Reed*
Daniel Webster	*John Varnum*
H. W. Dwight	*Aaron Hobart*
Edward Everett	*John Bailey*
John Locke	*John Davis*

To His Excellency, Governor Lincoln.

10

Copy of a letter from Hon. Mr. Lloyd to Governor Lincoln.

Washington, May 23, 1826.

Sir,—In accordance with the intention I had made known to you the last autumn, and the execution of which was then intermitted at the special request you were pleased to make, I have now the honor to inform you, I hereby resign my seat in the Senate of the United States.

A state of health not very firm, and which not being materially improved, rendering it doubtful if it would be in my power to devote that undivided and unceasing attention to the many and arduous duties devolving on the official station I have held, in a manner sufficiently useful to the Public, or acceptable to myself, have been among the leading inducements for my retiring from a situation alike elevated in itself, and endeared to me by many highly interesting associations. In communicating this information to the honourable Legislature, I pray you, Sir, to accompany it with an expression of the deep and grateful sense I entertain of the honor that has been conferred on me by repeated elections to an office of so much dignity and importance; and also with an aspiration to the Giver of every good gift, that the time-honored and enlighted Commonwealth of Massachusetts, first among the foremost in the assertion of our rights, and in the struggles of the Revolution; and whose foundations were so early and broadly laid, in the intelligence and patriotism of her Citizens, and the usefulness and equality of her Institutions, although shorn by her parental liberality of a large part of her territory, may long be distinguished by love of Country, by a fearless independence of opinion, and a marked adherence to her own rights, with a due respect for those of others; and replete with habits of morality, ample means of education, and a vigorous and successful enterprise and industry, ever be, and remain, a prominent and powerful Member of this great and most favored family of Republics.

With sentiments of the highest respect for your Excellency and the Legislature,

I have the honor to be, Sir, your and their

Ever Faithful and Obt. Svt.

JAMES LLOYD.

His Excellency Governor Lincoln.

Lightning Source UK Ltd.
Milton Keynes UK
UKHW021148061218
333419UK00013B/2020/P